Portraits of Jesus

life of Christ
through the Bible

6 GROUP BIBLE STUDIES FOR LENT

SELWYN HUGHES & MICHAEL ASHFORD

CWR, Waverley Abbey House, Waverley Lane, Farnham, Surrey GU9 8EP

UK: (and countries not listed below)
CWR, PO Box 230, Farnham, Surrey GU9 8XG.
Tel: (01252) 784710 Outside UK (44) 1252 784710

AUSTRALIA: CMC Australasia, PO Box 519, Belmont, Victoria 3216. Tel: (03) 5241 3288

CANADA: CMC Distribution Ltd, PO Box 7000, Niagara on the Lake, Ontario L0S 1J0.
Tel: (0800) 325 1297

GHANA: Challenge Enterprises of Ghana, PO Box 5723, Accra.
Tel: (021) 222437/223249 Fax: (021) 226227

HONG KONG: Cross Communications Ltd, 1/F, 562A Nathan Road, Kowloon.
Tel: 2780 1188 Fax: 2770 6229

INDIA: Crystal Communications, 10-3-18/4/1, East Marredpally, Secunderabad – 500 026.
Tel/Fax: (040) 7732801

KENYA: Keswick Bookshop, PO Box 10242, Nairobi. Tel: (02) 331692/226047

MALAYSIA: Salvation Book Centre (M) Sdn Bhd, 23 Jalan SS 2/64, 47300 Petaling Jaya, Selangor.
Tel: (03) 78766411/78766797 Fax: (03) 78757066/78756360

NEW ZEALAND: CMC New Zealand Ltd, Private Bag, 17910 Green Lane, Auckland.
Tel: (09) 5249393 Fax: (09) 5222137

NIGERIA: FBFM, Helen Baugh House, 96 St Finbarr's College Road, Akoka, Lagos.
Tel: (01) 7747429/4700218/825775/827264

PHILIPPINES: OMF Literature Inc, 776 Boni Avenue, Mandaluyong City.
Tel: (02) 531 2183 Fax: (02) 531 1960

REPUBLIC OF IRELAND: Scripture Union, 40 Talbot Street, Dublin 1.
Tel: (01) 8363764

SINGAPORE: Campus Crusade Asia Ltd, 315 Outram Road, 06-08 Tan Boon Liat Building,
Singapore 169074. Tel: (065) 222 3640

SOUTH AFRICA: Struik Christian Books, 80 MacKenzie Street, PO Box 1144, Cape Town 8000.
Tel: (021) 462 4360 Fax: (021) 461 3612

SRI LANKA: Christombu Books, 27 Hospital Street, Colombo 1.
Tel: (01) 433142/328909

TANZANIA: CLC Christian Book Centre, PO Box 1384, Mkwepu Street, Dar es Salaam.
Tel: (051) 2119439

UGANDA: New Day Bookshop, PO Box 2021, Kampala. Tel: (041) 255377

ZIMBABWE: Word of Life Books, Shop 4, Memorial Building, 35 S Machel Avenue, Harare.
Tel: (04) 781305 Fax: (04) 774739

For e-mail addresses, visit the CWR web site: **www.cwr.org.uk**

Portraits of Jesus

© CWR 2001 by Selwyn Hughes and Michael Ashford

Concept development, editing, design and production by CWR
Cover photograph: Roger Walker
Internal Photographs: Roger Walker
Printed in England by Linney Print
ISBN: 1-85345-189-4

Contents

Contents

Introduction

Why is this Lent Study Different?

Lent is a time of journeying with Jesus as He is heading to Jerusalem and the Cross. It is also a time of hope, a time of new life and the promise of resurrection. A number of Lent study books have focused on specific points in the story of Jesus, to enable people to reflect on His life and check if they are living as His followers.

This book uses a different focus – that of the lives of six biblical characters from the Old and New Testaments, each of who give us a picture of an aspect of Jesus' work in our salvation. It does however, aim to concentrate on bringing people to realise that what Jesus did during His life on earth has the most profound results for our lives today.

Seeing Pictures of Jesus

One saying from the ancient world was, "All roads lead to Rome". An even truer Christian statement is, "All truths of the Bible lead to Jesus."

The truths of the Old Testament all converge on Him and the truths of the New Testament all emerge from Him. Jesus can be considered as the hub of the Bible and the centre of gravity of the Scriptures.

There is an old adage (originally attributed to St Augustine) about the two Testaments that make up our Bible: The New is in the Old, concealed, the Old is in the New, revealed.

This points us to the principle that there are pictures we can see of Jesus "concealed" in the Old Testament, as well as illustrations of Him "revealed" in the New Testament.

Scripture is all about Jesus, and unless we understand this we will never properly understand the Bible.

There is a wonderful moment in the Book of Acts where Philip the Evangelist meets an Ethiopian eunuch on the road from Jerusalem to Gaza. The eunuch is reading the Book of Isaiah but cannot understand what it is about. Philip seizes his opportunity and shares "... that very passage of Scripture [Isaiah] and told him the good news about Jesus" (Acts 8:35).

Jesus is everywhere in the Bible. Wonderfully hidden in the "types" and "shadows", yet beautifully revealed to those who study the Scriptures as the key that unlocks them all.

Paul, in the first chapter of his Letter to the Colossians writes, "... in him all things hold together." In other words, Jesus is the key to everything on earth and in Heaven and, as the Living Word, the key to understanding the whole of the Bible.

The Bible paints wonderful pictures of many types of people. Some are bad, some are good. Some are ineffectual, others are towers of strength and power. Some walk with God, others turn against Him. And throughout the Bible there are people whose lives "mirror" episodes in the life of Jesus. This is called typology.

What is Typology?
Typology is the word that biblical scholars give to the way the Bible sets out the history of salvation, so that some of its earlier phases are seen as anticipations of later phases. In the language of typology, the earlier events constitute a "type" of the later.

So we should be able to see "types" or "pictures" of Jesus paralleled in the lives of characters in other parts of Bible. It is as though God is giving us a foretaste of the person and work of His Son throughout the pages of the whole Bible.

God's People

CWR's book, *God's People* leads its readers on a daily reading plan through the Bible in one year, following the lives of major characters in the Old and New Testaments. This Lent study course is based on the lives of six of the characters from that book:

- Isaac
- Joseph
- Esther
- Mary
- Stephen
- John

All of these people present us with aspects of Jesus' character and work in the accounts that the Bible gives us of their lives. Some of these aspects we can see apply directly to Jesus as God's Son, and enable us to grasp a particular viewpoint of His work of salvation. Other aspects we can apply to our lives today, and can provide the means for us to see what God wants from us.

This book is designed to be used for group study during the season of Lent – to prompt discussions about the Bible characters studied, and how their lives parallel, in part, that of Jesus.

Suggestions for Group Leaders

It is suggested that Group Leaders, rather than lead the whole session, encourage different Group Members to read the various elements – Opening and Closing Prayers, the Eye Opener, the Ice Breaker, the Bible Readings and the Introduction to the Character sections of the study. In this way Group Members can participate in the whole study, rather than just answering the questions. Indeed, a change of voice and pace can sometimes help other Group Members to concentrate better.

The Group Leader however, should facilitate the Questions section – having first read the relevant Background Notes on the study beforehand, and also lead the Final Thoughts section at the end of the study.

Suggestions for Group Members

Discussion groups are most effective and enjoyable when all members participate in an atmosphere of encouragement and respect. Arrive at your group meeting on time. Treat other Group Members as you would like to be treated. Listen attentively when they are speaking and encourage them. Be prepared to volunteer to read one of the different sections of the study. Be careful not to take more than your share of the group's time. Give each person an opportunity to speak.

Do not discuss anything shared in your group. It is important to maintain trust within the group. Pray that you will be open to what God will teach you through the study and through other group members. If you happen to need prayer or to share a personal problem, it is wise to do so privately with your Group Leader after the meeting has ended. If at all possible, let your Group Leader know of your need ahead of time.

Suggestions on Using This Book

Each study is designed to last a minimum of one hour and a maximum of one-and-half hours (timings for each section are suggested below).

Each study is divided into different sections. It is important that each section is used, as they are designed to lead Group Members through the study in a helpful, non-threatening way.

The different sections, comprising each study are:

- Opening Prayer
- Eye Opener
- Ice Breaker
- Bible Reading
- Introduction to the Bible Character
- Group Questions
- Final Thoughts
- Closing Prayer
- For Further Study

Opening Prayers (1 to 2 minutes)

Suggestions are given for the opening prayers for each study. These are purposely short prayers to enable Group Members who may not be used to praying in a small group setting to feel comfortable and to concentrate on the words of the prayers. Those leading prayers may substitute their own prayers if they feel led to do so.

Eye Openers (3 minutes)

These are designed to set the scene for the study and to arouse the Group Members' initial interest in the life of the Bible character.

Ice Breakers (10 minutes maximum)

The Ice Breakers are designed to encourage Group

Members to share their thoughts and experiences with one another in a non-threatening way. These are mainly (but not exclusively) light-hearted exercises to ease any initial unfamiliarity with other Group Members, and to promote conversation and participation before the main part of the study.

Bible Readings (5 minutes)
Some Group Members who may feel uncomfortable leading Prayers, Eye Openers or Ice Breakers may feel able to participate by reading the Bible passages for the group. In studies where there is more than one Bible passage, it is suggested that the readings be shared between two or more readers.

Introduction to the Character (10 minutes)
This section should be read out loud by one Group Member (or the Group Leader) so that all may follow the text.

Group Questions (45 minutes maximum)
The questions are designed so that all are used in the study, and structured so that the final question calls for Group Members to apply the teaching from the study to their own lives.

Discussions that go beyond the suggested questions are to be encouraged, providing they do not stray too far from the subject and use up the time allotted for the study. It is important that all the questions are asked and discussed. Group Leaders may need to exercise their authority to bring the Group Members back from a far-ranging discussion to the next question.

Final Thoughts (2 minutes)

This section should be read by the Group Leader to focus the group's thoughts on the truths revealed from the study.

Closing Prayers (1 to 2 minutes)

Suggestions are given for the closing prayers for each study. These are purposely short prayers to draw the study to a definite close. The Group Member leading prayers may substitute their own prayers if they feel led to do so.

For Further Study

These are suggestions for further study on the life of the character and other relevant Bible passages for members to use after the group meeting.

Leaders' Notes

There is a section of Leaders' Notes for each of the 6 studies at the end of this book. It is suggested that the Group Leader read the relevant section in preparation before each study.

Bibliography

Over 300 Red Hot Ice Breakers by Michael Puffett & Sheldon W. Rottler. Published by Monarch Books.

Isaac
Willing to be Sacrificed

Opening Prayer

Father, we thank You that we can meet during this period of Lent to come into Your presence to study Your Word. We pray for the guidance of Your Holy Spirit to lead our thoughts and our words down paths that You want to take us. Help us to see more of Your Son Jesus in our time together with You. In His name we pray. Amen.

Eye Opener

The name "Jesus" was chosen by God and means "The Lord saves". Jesus was being obedient to his Father's will and purpose to save mankind when He let Himself be led to the place of sacrifice – the Cross.

Paul says in his letter to the Philippians that Jesus, "... Who, being in very nature God, did not consider equality with God something to be grasped, but made himself nothing, taking the very nature of a servant, being made in human likeness. And being found in appearance as a man, he humbled himself and became obedient to death – even death on a cross!"

Ice Breaker "What's in a name?"

One lady's Christian name is Linda but from a very early age her father called her "Lindy-Lou". The last part of the name stuck and became her nickname. Today most people know her – not as Linda – but as Lou.

What nickname(s) have you been given in your life? Perhaps there are ones that please you or others that don't. Discuss with your group how you got the nickname and which people (if any) still call you by it.

Bible Reading

Genesis 22:1–19 (NIV)

Some time later God tested Abraham. He said to him, "Abraham!"

"Here I am," he replied.

Then God said, "Take your son, your only son, Isaac, whom you love, and go to the region of Moriah. Sacrifice him there as a burnt offering on one of the mountains I will tell you about."

Early the next morning Abraham got up and saddled his donkey. He took with him two of his servants and his son Isaac. When he had cut enough wood for the burnt offering, he set out for the place God had told him about. On the third day Abraham looked up and saw the place in the distance. He said to his servants, "Stay here with the donkey while I and the boy go over there. We will worship and then we will come back to you."

Abraham took the wood for the burnt offering and placed it on his son Isaac, and he himself carried the fire and the knife. As the two of them went on together, Isaac spoke up and said to his father Abraham, "Father?"

"Yes, my son?" Abraham replied.

"The fire and wood are here," Isaac said, "but where is the lamb for the burnt offering?"

Abraham answered, "God himself will provide the lamb for the burnt offering, my son." And the two of them went on together.

When they reached the place God had told him about, Abraham built an altar there and arranged the wood on it. He bound his son Isaac and laid him on the altar, on top of the wood. Then he reached out his hand and took the knife to slay his son. But the angel of the Lord called out to him from heaven, "Abraham! Abraham!"

"Here I am," he replied.

"Do not lay a hand on the boy," he said. "Do not do anything to him. Now I know that you fear God, because you have not withheld from me your son, your only son."

Abraham looked up and there in a thicket he saw a ram caught by its horns. He went over and took the ram and sacrificed it as a burnt offering instead of his son. So Abraham called that place "The Lord Will Provide". And to this day it is said, "On the mountain of the Lord it will be provided."

The angel of the Lord called to Abraham from heaven a second time and said, "I swear by myself, declares the Lord, that because you have done this and have not withheld your son, your only son, I will surely bless you and make your descendants as numerous as the stars in the sky and as the sand on the seashore. Your descendants will take possession of the cities of their enemies, and through your offspring all nations on earth will be blessed, because you have obeyed me."

Then Abraham returned to his servants, and they set off together for Beersheba. And Abraham stayed in Beersheba.

Introduction to Isaac's Submission

When we read about the amazing life of Isaac's father Abraham, we see that Isaac was the product of a miracle – conceived and born when Abraham and his mother Sarah were very elderly. Sarah was so disbelieving when told she would bear a child in her old age, she laughed. Before the baby was born God selected the name Isaac (meaning "Laughter"), to remind Sarah never again to doubt God's power.

Because we can't see God, some people don't believe in His power – or that He even cares about mankind. One mother, seeing her young daughter painting a picture of a face, asked whose portrait it was. "It's God," answered the girl. "But no-one knows what God looks like," her mother said. Unperturbed, the youngster replied, "They will when I've finished my picture."

In our Bible passage, Abraham receives the divine
command to take his only son Isaac, and offer him as a
human sacrifice. Now surely there is no way God can
justify the murder of an innocent child? Well, whatever the
reason for the strange request, Abraham (the "friend of
God", as James calls him; James 2:23) is quick to obey.
The Patriarch could have been forgiven if he had waited
a few days to think through the ramifications of God's
command, but the Scripture tells us that Abraham got up
early the next morning and set out to implement God's
wishes.

Bible commentators believe, and Jewish tradition is, that
Isaac was around thirty years of age when he let himself
be prepared for sacrifice and could have easily over-
powered his aging father. Abraham's reference to his son
as "boy" causes us to think of Isaac as a child, but given
Abraham's age this could be simply a term of endear-
ment. The sacrifice took place on Mount Moriah; today
we know this high place as Mount Zion (the Temple
Mount) in Jerusalem. Jesus' death took place less than a
mile away on Calvary.

At the end of our Bible reading, when Isaac is placed on
the altar and Abraham takes the knife in his hand and is
ready to plunge it into the body of his dear son, God
intervenes. Enough was accomplished in this incident to
depict to Abraham, and to succeeding generations, that
this was a dress rehearsal for a greater sacrifice that
would one day take place in the very same vicinity.

Already we may see parallels in the life of Isaac and of
Jesus as willing sacrifices, so let's look at some questions
that might help us see even more.

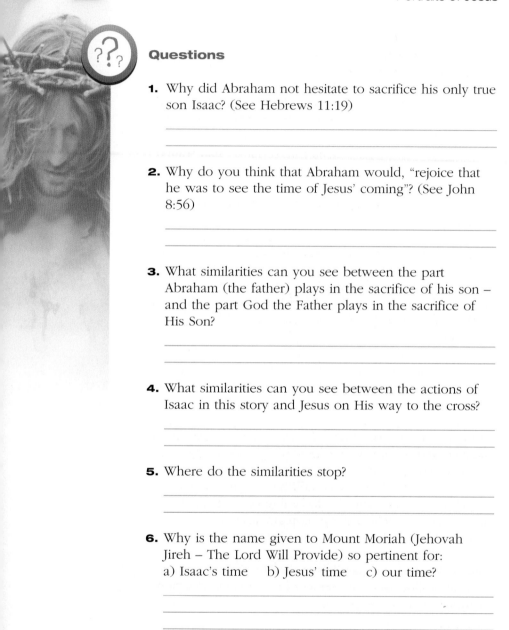

Questions

1. Why did Abraham not hesitate to sacrifice his only true son Isaac? (See Hebrews 11:19)

_____

_____

2. Why do you think that Abraham would, "rejoice that he was to see the time of Jesus' coming"? (See John 8:56)

_____

_____

3. What similarities can you see between the part Abraham (the father) plays in the sacrifice of his son – and the part God the Father plays in the sacrifice of His Son?

_____

_____

4. What similarities can you see between the actions of Isaac in this story and Jesus on His way to the cross?

_____

_____

5. Where do the similarities stop?

_____

_____

6. Why is the name given to Mount Moriah (Jehovah Jireh – The Lord Will Provide) so pertinent for:
a) Isaac's time   b) Jesus' time   c) our time?

_____

_____

_____

7. What difference do you think Jesus' willing sacrifice has made for your life?

_____

8. What else has God provided in your life that you could thank Him for today?

Final Thoughts

If Jesus had not been willing to be the sacrifice for our sins, where would that leave us? We could never go to church enough times, or sing enough hymns, or offer enough prayers, or do enough good deeds to make amends for all the wrong actions we've done, or the wrong words we've spoken, or the wrong thoughts that we've had in our lives. These wrongs distance us from God – only a perfect life could pay the price He demands for sin. Praise God that He was willing to sacrifice His one and only Son Jesus, to bring us back to Him.

Closing Prayer

O Father, help us in times of doubt, to doubt our doubts and believe our beliefs. Help us to choose what is right, no matter how many influences work in our hearts to the contrary. Thank You for allowing Your Son to be the willing sacrifice for our sins. May we express our heartfelt thanks today, not only with our lips, but also with our lives. For the sake of Jesus, our Saviour and Lord. Amen.

For Further Study

Isaiah Ch 53; John 1:29; 1 Peter 1:19; 2:21–25
What did Isaiah prophesy?
How did John and Peter confirm this?

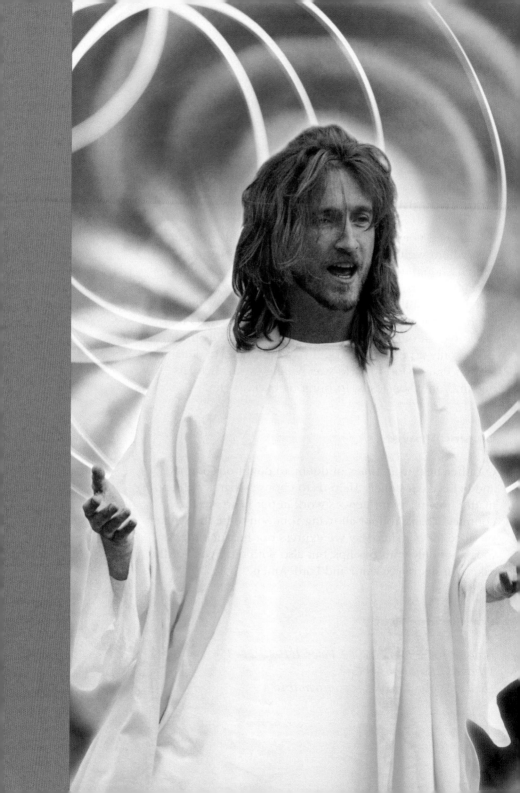

Joseph
Redeeming the Lost

Opening Prayer

Father, we thank You that again we can meet with You during Lent as we study Your Word. We pray that You would come and take Your place as head of our meeting and that Your Holy Spirit would direct our thoughts, our words and our feelings for each other. Help us once again to learn more of Your Son Jesus today. In His name we pray. Amen.

Eye Opener

The description of the gift of Jacob to his favourite son Joseph – the "many coloured" coat, is generally acknowledged to be mistranslated from the original Hebrew. A more accurate translation would be "long sleeved" coat. The significance of this description is that it would have been the other brothers who wore short sleeved tunics and did the work on the homestead. Jacob therefore, appointed Joseph as "foreman" and he told his brothers what to do.

You can imagine how popular this made Joseph with them!

Ice Breaker "Mistaken Identity"

A man bore such an uncanny physical resemblance to a famously reclusive film star, he was always being mistaken for him in public. Tiring of constantly denying he was the film star, the man taught himself how to duplicate the star's signature and made fans happy by signing their autograph books

The publicity-shy actor heard about the man, interviewed him and finally hired him to take his place at various

*public functions. It is even rumoured it was the double
who collected the film star's Oscar at the Academy Awards
ceremony.*

*Has anyone ever mistaken your identity? Discuss with
your group how the mix-up occurred and what the
consequences were.*

Bible Readings

Genesis 44:1–17

Now Joseph gave these instructions to the steward of his
house: "Fill the men's sacks with as much food as they
can carry, and put each man's silver in the mouth of his
sack. Then put my cup, the silver one, in the mouth of
the youngest one's sack, along with the silver for his
grain." And he did as Joseph said.

As morning dawned, the men were sent on their way
with their donkeys. They had not gone far from the city
when Joseph said to his steward, "Go after those men at
once, and when you catch up with them, say to them,
'Why have you repaid good with evil? Isn't this the cup
my master drinks from and also uses for divination? This
is a wicked thing you have done.'"

When he caught up with them, he repeated these
words to them. But they said to him, "Why does my lord
say such things? Far be it from your servants to do
anything like that! We even brought back to you from the
land of Canaan the silver we found inside the mouths of
our sacks. So why would we steal silver or gold from
your master's house? If any of your servants is found to
have it, he will die; and the rest of us will become my
lord's slaves."

"Very well, then," he said, "let it be as you say.
Whoever is found to have it will become my slave; the
rest of you will be free from blame."

Each of them quickly lowered his sack to the ground and opened it. Then the steward proceeded to search, beginning with the oldest and ending with the youngest. And the cup was found in Benjamin's sack. At this, they tore their clothes. Then they all loaded their donkeys and returned to the city.

Joseph was still in the house when Judah and his brothers came in, and they threw themselves to the ground before him. Joseph said to them, "What is this you have done? Don't you know that a man like me can find things out by divination?"

"What can we say to my lord?" Judah replied. "What can we say? How can we prove our innocence? God has uncovered your servants' guilt. We are now my lord's slaves – we ourselves and the one who was found to have the cup."

But Joseph said, "Far be it from me to do such a thing! Only the man who was found to have the cup will become my slave. The rest of you, go back to your father in peace."

Genesis 45:1–7

Then Joseph could no longer control himself before all his attendants, and he cried out, "Make everyone leave my presence!" So there was no-one with Joseph when he made himself known to his brothers. And he wept so loudly that the Egyptians heard him, and Pharaoh's household heard about it.

Joseph said to his brothers, "I am Joseph! Is my father still living?" But his brothers were not able to answer him, because they were terrified at his presence.

Then Joseph said to his brothers, "Come close to me." When they had done so, he said, "I am your brother Joseph, the one you sold into Egypt! And now, do not be distressed and do not be angry with yourselves for selling me here, because it was to save lives that God sent me ahead of you. For two years now there has been famine in the land, and for the next five years there will not be ploughing and reaping. But God sent me ahead of you to preserve for you a remnant on earth and to save your lives by a great deliverance."

Introduction to the story of Joseph

The story of Joseph is unquestionably one of the most thrilling in all of Scripture, and records his life in more detail than that of the lives of other great Patriarchs such as Abraham and Isaac. Most Bible scholars believe that this is because Joseph typifies, more than any other Bible personality, the life and character of our Lord Jesus Christ.

Joseph is the favourite son of his father Jacob, yet he is betrayed by his brothers and sold for twenty pieces of silver as a slave.

Joseph is carried to Egypt where the wife of his new master attempts to seduce him. When he resists her temptations, she falsely accuses Joseph and he is sent to prison. When Pharaoh starts having dreams, Joseph interprets them as foreshadowing times of great plenty followed by great famine. Joseph is released from prison and elevated to the position of Minister of Agriculture to prepare for the coming events.

(You could say that Joseph was the straightest man in the Bible, because Pharaoh made a "ruler" out of him!)

With the famine at its height, Joseph's brothers come to Egypt seeking food but fail to recognise their brother. He sets up a situation – albeit initially painful for the brothers – that gives them the chance to make amends for their sins against him, and provides Joseph with the opportunity to reveal to them his true identity.

There are two possible explanations for Joseph saying that he practised divination using the cup he had hidden in Benjamin's sack. The first is that it was literally true, cup divination was certainly practised in ancient Egypt according to scholars. The second, and more likely explanation is that Joseph wanted to frighten his brothers even more by emphasising their guilt, and indicating that he had powers to see events past, present and future.

Whatever the explanation, Joseph was certainly one of the few people who were able to maintain their spiritual poise at the peak of success, as well as in the midst of trouble. His tremendous organisational ability, his patience through tribulation, his faithfulness in fame and success and his forgiving spirit are all tributes to his character.

Yet what stands out above all else, is his conviction that God has a specific purpose for his life, and neither the betrayal of his brothers nor the temptations offered by an evil woman could interfere with that purpose. He moved forward in the quiet conviction that his life was not merely a succession of coincidences, but was being directed by a loving God.

At the end of the Bible story of Joseph, he not only pardons his brothers for their sins against him, but also redeems them from their pitiful state and buys them some of the best land in Egypt. This foreshadows the pardon we receive from Jesus for our sins and the redemption He offers as a free gift of God.

Let's look at some questions that might help to reveal other parallels between the life and actions of Joseph and the life and work of Jesus Christ.

Questions

1. What parallel can you see between Joseph's words to his brothers "I am Joseph" and similar words spoken by the Son of God to Saul on the Damascus road? (See Acts 9:5)

_____

_____

_____

2. What similarities can you see between Joseph raised from the prison house of darkness and despair, to the highest place in the kingdom and the events in Jesus' life? (See Philippians 2:8–10)

_____

_____

_____

3. Joseph – like Jesus – was rejected, tempted, slandered and falsely accused yet never once yielded to self pity. What motivation in their lives do you think caused this?

_____

_____

_____

4. What prompted Joseph's brother Judah, to sell him for twenty pieces of silver? What do you think prompted Judas to "sell" Jesus for a similar but slightly greater amount?

_____

_____

_____

_____

5. When Joseph's brothers met him in Egypt they failed to recognise him. What similar occasions such as this can you think of in the life of Jesus?

_____

_____

_____

6. On which occasion did Jesus reveal Himself to His disciples as He really was? (See Matthew 17:1–5)

_____

_____

_____

7. Can you recall an instance in your life where God has revealed Himself to you?

_____

_____

_____

8. What can you thank God for that He has done for you?

_____

_____

_____

Final Thoughts

Jesus said that He came to "seek and save the lost". How "lost" were you when Jesus found you? God has given us a Redeemer in Jesus, who has purchased for us God's greatest gift – His Grace. We can't buy this gift, anymore than we can buy someone's love. It has to be freely given and freely accepted. But it is the greatest gift that anyone can ever receive because it leads to eternal life.

Closing Prayer

O Father, forgive us when we fail to reveal Your true identity to others through our words and deeds. Help us to remember that in Jesus we have someone who has revealed You to us and shown us what You are like – a God of love and mercy. Thank You for sending Your Son to show us how much You love each one of us by offering Your pardon and redemption as a free gift. May we express that love back to You. For the sake of Jesus, our Redeemer. Amen.

For Further Study

1. *Although Jesus was rejected and outlawed by the religious leaders of his day, on three separate occasions God honoured His Son by speaking from heaven with words of the highest commendation. Find them in Matthew 3:17, Luke 9:35 and John 12:28*

2. *There are at least 16 major parallels between the life of Joseph and of Jesus. You'll find them listed in the CWR publication,* God's People *by Selwyn Hughes and Trevor J Partridge.*

Esther
Saving her People

Opening Prayer

Heavenly Father, thank You in this time of Lent that we can gather together to consider Your Son, Jesus and His work of salvation for us. We ask for the help of Your Holy Spirit in our meeting today to open our minds and our thoughts to what You want to teach us through our Bible study. Grant us patience and love for each other as we meet in Jesus' name. Amen.

Eye Opener

Jesus was following God's purpose for His life when He set out on the road to Jerusalem and His death. He completely surrendered His will to the will of His Father when He prayed in the garden of Gethsemane, "Not my will, but your will be done."

Today, every time we say the words of the Lord's Prayer, "Your will be done on earth as it is in heaven" we are submitting to this principle.

In this study we will be looking at the life of Esther who submitted to this same principle and ended up saving her people from extermination. So significant do the Jewish people regard this event, that they celebrate Esther's act in one of their major feasts – even today!

Ice Breaker

Each member of the group picks a number between 2 and 9 which they keep to themselves. Multiply this number by 9. Add together the two digits of the answer.
Subtract 5 from that number. Translate that number into a corresponding letter of the alphabet. If your number is 1,

*your letter is A; if your number is 2, your letter is B, etc.
Chose a foreign country beginning with that letter. Take
the second letter of that country and chose an animal
beginning with that letter. Now think of the colour of that
animal.*

*Every member of the group should now be thinking of the
same-coloured animal and the same country. What is it?*

*Note: The whole purpose of this exercise is to lead everyone
from potentially different starting points down a particular
route to the common final destination of naming the
same-coloured specific animal and a single country.*

*Now let's look at one example from the Bible in which God
leads people to His purposes.*

Bible Reading

Esther 3:13–4:17

Dispatches were sent by couriers to all the king's
provinces with the order to destroy, kill and annihilate all
the Jews – young and old, women and little children – on
a single day, the thirteenth day of the twelfth month, the
month of Adar, and to plunder their goods. A copy of the
text of the edict was to be issued as law in every
province and made known to the people of every nation-
ality so that they would be ready for that day.

Spurred on by the king's command, the couriers went
out, and the edict was issued in the citadel of Susa. The
king and Haman sat down to drink, but the city of Susa
was bewildered.

When Mordecai learned of all that had been done, he
tore his clothes, put on sackcloth and ashes, and went out
into the city, wailing loudly and bitterly. But he went only
as far as the king's gate, because no-one clothed in sack-

cloth was allowed to enter it. In every province to which the edict and order of the king came, there was great mourning among the Jews, with fasting, weeping and wailing. Many lay in sackcloth and ashes.

When Esther's maids and eunuchs came and told her about Mordecai, she was in great distress. She sent clothes for him to put on instead of his sackcloth, but he would not accept them. Then Esther summoned Hathach, one of the king's eunuchs assigned to attend her, and ordered him to find out what was troubling Mordecai and why.

So Hathach went out to Mordecai in the open square of the city in front of the king's gate. Mordecai told him everything that had happened to him, including the exact amount of money Haman had promised to pay into the royal treasury for the destruction of the Jews. He also gave him a copy of the text of the edict for their annihilation, which had been published in Susa, to show to Esther and explain it to her, and he told him to urge her to go into the king's presence to beg for mercy and plead with him for her people.

Hathach went back and reported to Esther what Mordecai had said. Then she instructed him to say to Mordecai, "All the king's officials and the people of the royal provinces know that for any man or woman who approaches the king in the inner court without being summoned the king has but one law: that he be put to death. The only exception to this is for the king to extend the gold sceptre to him and spare his life. But thirty days have passed since I was called to go to the king."

When Esther's words were reported to Mordecai, he sent back this answer: "Do not think that because you are in the king's house you alone of all the Jews will escape. For if you remain silent at this time, relief and deliverance for the Jews will arise from another place, but you and your father's family will perish. And who knows but that you have come to royal position for such a time as this?"

Then Esther sent this reply to Mordecai: "Go, gather

together all the Jews who are in Susa, and fast for me. Do not eat or drink for three days, night or day. I and my maids will fast as you do. When this is done, I will go to the king, even though it is against the law. And if I perish, I perish."

So Mordecai went away and carried out all of Esther's instructions.

Introduction to Esther

The story of Esther begins in the palace of the Persian King Xerxes, who summons his wife Queen Vashti to appear before an assembled company at the end of a great feast to show off her beauty. This she refuses to do, and is promptly disposed of by the angry despot. His courtiers urge him to choose a successor to Vashti, and a "Miss Persia" beauty contest is held for him to select his new queen. He chooses an orphaned Jewess called Hadassah, who we now know by her later name, Esther – who had been adopted and raised by her cousin Mordecai.

When Esther has been crowned queen, Mordecai over-hears a plot against the king's life and informs Esther who, in turn, conveys the information to the king. After investigation the two conspirators are convicted and hanged – the whole affair being recorded in the official archives.
King Xerxes promotes an Agagite by the name of Haman to be his Prime Minister, decreeing that everyone should acknowledge his prominent position by bowing down before him. This Mordecai refuses to do, explaining that as a Jew he cannot bow down before anyone but God.

Enraged, Haman determines to destroy, not only Mordecai, but every Jew in the Persian Empire and

persuades the king to issue a decree calling for the massacre of all the Jews. Mordecai pleads with Esther to intercede with the king, telling her this could well be the divine reason why she is in the royal palace. Haman meanwhile, has already built a gallows on which to hang Mordecai.

At night Xerxes is unable to sleep and asks that the court archives be read to him. During the reading, he hears of Mordecai's part in foiling the assassination attempt on his life, and gives orders for Mordecai to be publicly honoured in a feast. Haman, to his dismay, is obliged to enter into the celebrations.

At the feast Esther boldly denounces Haman, courageously identifies herself with her doomed people, and pleads with the king to save them from destruction. The king, in great anger, orders Haman to be executed on the very gallows which he had built for Mordecai. Now that Mordecai's relationship with Esther is out in the open, he is summoned by the king who appoints him as Haman's successor.

Although Haman is now dead, the decree he inspired against the Jews still stands. Queen Esther tearfully and eloquently pleads with the king for her people to be spared. He issues another decree authorising the Jews to defend themselves against any attacks made arising from the first edict, and as a result 75,000 of their enemies perish.

In her day, Esther was anointed queen so that God's will might direct her life to save her people from annihilation. The Jews still celebrate their mighty deliverance, calling the celebration "The Feast of Purim", and they read the book of Esther every year at that time.

We are remembering Jesus during this time of Lent as the anointed Christ, who by following God's will for His life, is saving people all over the world even today.

Questions

1. Esther is the only book in the Bible in which the name of God is not mentioned. What evidence can you see of His guiding hand in our Bible reading? (See also Romans 8:28)

_____

_____

_____

2. Although Esther held the high office of queen, she didn't put on "airs and graces" and she was unselfish in her love and loyalty towards her people. How does Jesus' attitude compare? (See Philippians 2:7)

_____

_____

_____

3. Esther chose a course of terrible danger to herself for the sake of her people. How does this compare with the course God chose for Jesus?

_____

_____

_____

4. Esther had a deep sense of destiny in her life – as Mordecai reminded her, that she had "come to royal position for such a time as this" (Esther 4:14). How would you compare this with Jesus' sense of destiny?

_____

_____

_____

5. Esther, as the anointed queen, became the saviour of her people. How did Jesus, the anointed King, save His people?

_____

_____

6. It might seem irrelevant that after the hanging of the two conspirators in the assassination attempt, all the details of the event were written down. But God worked through this apparent irrelevancy. Has anything similar happened in your life?

_____

_____

_____

7. We learn from Esther's life that God's timing is punctual and perfect (See Galatians 4:4–5). Can you think of a time in your life when God's timing has been punctual and/or perfect?

_____

_____

_____

Final Thoughts

Jesus saves His people by standing before God on their behalf on the Day of Judgment. If we were to attempt to defend ourselves on that day, everyone of us would be found guilty. Yet those who have followed Jesus will find that they have the greatest defence lawyer in the universe speaking for them on that day. The verdict at our trial will be "not guilty" because He has taken our condemnation when He suffered for our sins on the cross and He will intercede on our behalf. The promise of the Bible is that Jesus continues to intercede for us in this life too. What a wonderful Saviour we have in Him.

Closing Prayer

Heavenly Father, we just wonder with amazement that You are the sovereign light behind everything, and that nothing can separate us from Your love. Help us to continue to learn in this time of Lent from the life of Jesus and to see Your plans behind everything that happens to us. Give us Your insight to see Your purpose in all the pathways in which You lead us. In the name of Jesus, our Way, our Truth and our Life. Amen.

For Further Study

Esther's intercession (Esther 7:3 & 4) is a model on which we as Christians, can safely build. She is bold, simple, plain and direct (see Proverbs 28:1). "All intercession," it has been said, "starts with identification". It begins when we allow the groan of God to enter our own souls.

Mary
Trusting in God

Opening Prayer

Almighty God, we are grateful for the times of study we have shared together during this period of Lent and the way in which You have shown us pictures of Your Son, Jesus, in the lives of people from the Bible. Help us today to see yet another aspect of Jesus as we look at the life of His mother, Mary. Send Your Holy Spirit to guide our thoughts and words. In Jesus' name. Amen.

Eye Opener

Mary's simple faith in the power and goodness of God, combined with her humble duties of home, motherhood and family mark her out as one of the greatest, if not the greatest women who has ever lived.

Yet Mary was probably no more than fourteen or fifteen years old when she was visited by the archangel, who told her she was to bear a child. Although she was betrothed to Joseph, they were not yet married and Jewish Law proscribed that women who got pregnant out of wedlock should be stoned to death!

Do you know any teenagers around Mary's age? How do you think they would cope with the news the archangel brought Mary?

Ice-breaker

Four people are travelling in a hot air balloon; a drug-addicted pop star, a church minister who has lost his faith, a pregnant prostitute and a young child with an incurable disease. The balloon sustains irreparable damage and will only carry the weight of one person.

Discuss with your group which three people ought to be sacrificed to save the life of the remaining one?

Bible Readings

Luke 2:34–35

The child's father and mother marvelled at what was said about him. Then Simeon blessed them and said to Mary, his mother: "This child is destined to cause the falling and rising of many in Israel, and to be a sign that will be spoken against, so that the thoughts of many hearts will be revealed. And a sword will pierce your own soul too."

John 2:1–11

On the third day a wedding took place at Cana in Galilee. Jesus' mother was there, and Jesus and his disciples had also been invited to the wedding. When the wine was gone, Jesus' mother said to him, "They have no more wine."

"Dear woman, why do you involve me?" Jesus replied. "My time has not yet come."

His mother said to the servants, "Do whatever he tells you."

Nearby stood six stone water jars, the kind used by the Jews for ceremonial washing, each holding from twenty to thirty gallons.

Jesus said to the servants, "Fill the jars with water"; so they filled them to the brim.

Then he told them, "Now draw some out and take it to the master of the banquet."

They did so, and the master of the banquet tasted the water that had been turned into wine. He did not realise where it had come from, though the servants who had drawn the water knew. Then he called the bridegroom aside and said, "Everyone brings out the choice wine first and then the cheaper wine after the guests have had too

much to drink; but you have saved the best till now."

This, the first of his miraculous signs, Jesus performed in Cana of Galilee. He thus revealed his glory, and his disciples put their faith in him.

Mark 3:20–21 and 31–35

Then Jesus entered a house, and again a crowd gathered, so that he and his disciples were not even able to eat. When his family heard about this, they went to take charge of him, for they said, "He is out of his mind."

Then Jesus' mother and brothers arrived. Standing outside, they sent someone in to call him. A crowd was sitting around him, and they told him, "Your mother and brothers are outside looking for you."

"Who are my mother and my brothers?" he asked.

Then he looked at those seated in a circle around him and said, "Here are my mother and brothers! Whoever does God's will is my brother and sister and mother."

John 19:25–27

Near the cross of Jesus stood his mother, his mother's sister, Mary the wife of Clopas, and Mary Magdalene. When Jesus saw his mother there, and the disciple whom he loved standing near by, he said to his mother, "Dear woman, here is your son," and to the disciple, "Here is your mother." From that time on, this disciple took her into his home.

Acts 1:13–14

When they arrived, they went upstairs to the room where they were staying. Those present were Peter, John, James and Andrew; Philip and Thomas, Bartholomew and Matthew; James son of Alphaeus and Simon the Zealot, and Judas son of James. They all joined together constantly in prayer, along with the women and Mary the mother of Jesus, and with his brothers.

Introduction to Mary

Mary's role as the mother of Jesus was something that God ordained. He entrusted a lowly girl from a poor family, possibly no more than fifteen, who lived in an almost forgotten backwater of Israel, to bear His Son. And He chose her because of the willingness of her heart to accept God's will and make an enormous sacrifice that, given the strict moral ethics of the Jews, could have cost her not just her future husband, Joseph, but also her life.

Mary saw from the very beginning the greatness of God's divine purpose being fulfilled, and remained faithful in response as it gradually developed before her. In the Gospel stories we learn of Mary talking with God, conceiving a son by His Holy Spirit and visiting her relatives to express her joy at God favouring her so greatly. We witness her giving birth to Jesus in the stable in Bethlehem, and a few days later consecrating Him at the Temple in Jerusalem.

Then we read of her travels with her husband and child to Egypt, before returning with them to Nazareth. We share her concern when the family visit Jerusalem and discover the twelve-year-old boy missing on the return journey.

Years later, when Jesus had grown into manhood we see her asking Him to use His powers at the wedding in Cana. Later we see her in Jerusalem weeping beside His cross as He endured the pain of His sacrifice for sin.

Finally, after gathering with His disciples in the Upper Room at Pentecost, she experiences the work of the Holy Spirit again – this time turning Jesus' followers into powerful preachers and healers able to win converts and do miracles in the Son's name.

There are many lessons we can learn from Mary's life. But perhaps the most important, is that despite the sadness and sorrow she suffered because of her relationship to Jesus Christ, she determined to draw even closer to God. There is a picture of Jesus here in His mother's life, that shows how to combine down-to-earth relationships with others, with an acceptance to make any sacrifice that God demands on their behalf.

The Gospels call Mary "highly favoured", not just because of her privileged position in her relationship with the Son of God, but also because of her willingness to sacrifice everything in her acceptance of God's will for her life.

Mary's trust in God's plan for her life, gives us a picture of Jesus' trust in God's plan for His life. Let's look at some questions that may help explain that shared trust in God's purposes.

Questions

1. When Jesus was born, Mary was told that she would experience not only great honour, but also great sorrow? (see Luke 2:35). Which do you think came first?

_____

_____

_____

2. What do you think led Mary to tell the servants during the crisis that developed at the wedding feast in Cana "Do whatever he tells you"? (See John 2:5)

_____

_____

_____

3. Mary would have met Jesus' disciples during His ministry. Do you think she approved of them?

_____

_____

_____

4. When Mary went with Jesus' family and friends to try to restrain Him over what they saw as a developing religious mania, what do you think she felt at Jesus' response? (See Mark 3:21 & 31–35)

_____

_____

_____

5. Can you express what you think Mary's feelings might have been when she stood at the foot the Cross, seeing the fire of life fade from Jesus' eyes and hearing His cry, "My God, my God, why have you forsaken me?" (See Matthew 27:46)

_____

_____

_____

6. Why do you think she was still in company of the disciples in the Upper Room at Pentecost? (See Acts 1:14)

_____

_____

_____

7. What do people you know put their trust in today? Can you share with the group what they are?

_____

_____

_____

8. Is there an area of your life that you feel God could be calling you to trust Him more for in the future?

_____

_____

_____

Final Thoughts

Jesus trusted God with His life to the point of death and beyond. Whether Jesus was healing, driving out demons, performing great miracles, or walking into dangerous situations, He trusted His Father implicitly. Even in the Garden of Gethsemane, having prayed that if possible, "the cup [of suffering for sin] be taken from me", He still trusted God enough to say, "yet not my will, but yours be done."

Can we bring ourselves to trust God for everything? Our clothes, our food, our homes, our families – even our lives? The evidence from the lives of the great saints of the Church, is that when we do trust God for everything, He will use us for His purposes to bring about the greatest good.

Closing Prayer

Dear Heavenly Father, You have allowed us to see the lovely character of Mary and the trust she showed in You for Your purpose for her life. Thank you that she showed the same trust in Jesus. Help us to see that, through His trust in You, Jesus was willing to endure death on the Cross and give Himself for each one of us to bring us ultimately to You. For His name's sake. Amen.

For Further Study

Mary's hymn of praise to God is called The Magnificat – the word comes from the same root as "magnify" (see Luke 2:46–55). Read it to get a big, "magnified" picture of God.

"Godliness" says a Christian commentator, "is acting as God would do if He were in your shoes." How difficult it is to see everything that happens to us from God's perspective – but how marvellous it is when we overcome that difficulty and learn to see life from His point of view (see 1 Peter 3:3–5).

Stephen
Forgiving his Enemies

Opening Prayer

Heavenly Father, thank You for this opportunity You have given us to meet with You during the season of Lent. We ask that You would be in our thoughts, our words and our deeds as we look at a section of Your Word to us. Help us to see more of Your Son, Jesus, in our time together. We pray in His name and for His sake. Amen.

Eye Opener

Stephen was the first of those selected by the Apostles in the early Church in Jerusalem, to do the work of a server or "deacon". One of Stephen's tasks was to ensure that the widows in the church were cared for. There were two groups of widows in the early Church, and those from a Gentile (Greek) background, complained they weren't getting a fair share of food compared with the Jewish widows. It is interesting that Stephen, and all the first deacons appointed to deal with this, have Greek names!

Much of Stephen's work however, was interrupted by the outbreak of violent persecution against Christians. As it turned out, Stephen was not only the first deacon in the early Church but also its first martyr.

Ice Breaker

God has the ability to forgive your sins – and then, most amazingly, to forget them. Someone once described this in terms of God taking all your sins, putting them into a big sack, tying the end and then throwing the sack into the middle of a huge lake. Finally, as the ripples die away, God puts a large sign in the water that carries the words, "No Fishing!"

We know however, that it is difficult to forgive and even harder to forget when someone has wronged us or those we love. Can you share with your group a time when you felt you were wronged and if you have been able to forgive?

Bible Readings

Acts 6:8–15; 7:1–3

Now Stephen, a man full of God's grace and power, did great wonders and miraculous signs among the people. Opposition arose, however, from members of the Synagogue of the Freedmen (as it was called) – Jews of Cyrene and Alexandria as well as the provinces of Cilicia and Asia. These men began to argue with Stephen, but they could not stand up against his wisdom or the Spirit by whom he spoke.

Then they secretly persuaded some men to say, "We have heard Stephen speak words of blasphemy against Moses and against God."

So they stirred up the people and the elders and the teachers of the law. They seized Stephen and brought him before the Sanhedrin. They produced false witnesses, who testified, "This fellow never stops speaking against this holy place and against the law. For we have heard him say that this Jesus of Nazareth will destroy this place and change the customs Moses handed down to us."

All who were sitting in the Sanhedrin looked intently at Stephen, and they saw that his face was like the face of an angel.

Then the high priest asked him, "Are these charges true?" To this he replied: "Brothers and fathers, listen to me! The God of glory appeared to our father Abraham while he was still in Mesopotamia, before he lived in Haran. 'Leave your country and your people,' God said, 'and go to the land I will show you.'"

Acts 7:51–60 and 8:1

"You stiff-necked people, with uncircumcised hearts and ears! You are just like your fathers: You always resist the Holy Spirit! Was there ever a prophet your fathers did not persecute? They even killed those who predicted the coming of the Righteous One. And now you have betrayed and murdered him – you who have received the law that was put into effect through angels but have not obeyed it."

When they heard this, they were furious and gnashed their teeth at him. But Stephen, full of the Holy Spirit, looked up to heaven and saw the glory of God, and Jesus standing at the right hand of God. "Look," he said, "I see heaven open and the Son of Man standing at the right hand of God."

At this they covered their ears and, yelling at the top of their voices, they all rushed at him, dragged him out of the city and began to stone him. Meanwhile, the witnesses laid their clothes at the feet of a young man named Saul.

While they were stoning him, Stephen prayed, "Lord Jesus, receive my spirit." Then he fell on his knees and cried out, "Lord, do not hold this sin against them." When he had said this, he fell asleep.

And Saul was there, giving approval to his death.

Introduction to Stephen

Many commentators believe that Stephen is the central figure in the New Testament, between Jesus and Paul. His character and abilities are of the highest order. Not only is he Spirit-filled, but he is also a man of great faith and power.

His ministry in and around Jerusalem is such, that wherever he goes signs and wonders accompany the preaching of the Word. So powerful is the impact of Stephen's life and service for God on the community that the Jewish leaders become fearful of him.

They arrest Stephen and when given the chance to speak, he gives one of the finest sermons in the whole of Scripture. In "true" preaching construction, it even has three main points! – What is true worship? What is true ministry? What is the truth about Jesus?

This sermon is cut short by the mob who are out for blood. They seize Stephen and take him outside the city to kill him. The place, his mode of death, the stones thrown by the witnesses, are all in exact accordance with ancient precedent laid out in Jewish law (see Leviticus 24:13–16). By such formalities the executioners seek to represent their evil work as a solemn enactment of national law upon a blasphemer of Jehovah. Stephen's death however, is his last act of imitation of his Lord. He catches for a brief time, the glory of his departed Lord – and reflecting it, is transformed into the same image.

His life seems so possessed by the Holy Spirit, and Christ's nature is so clearly seen in his character, that it is not surprising the Christ-rejecting Jews put him to death.

Stephen's open forgiveness of this crime against him, gives us a parallel to the forgiveness of Jesus for those who put Him to death. Let's look at some questions that may show us other parallels between Stephen's forgiving attitude and Jesus' divine forgiveness.

Questions

1. Did you notice the description of Stephen given at the
start of our Bible reading: "full of grace and power"? Is
it possible to be full of grace and have little power? Or
to be full of power but have only a little grace? What
do you think?

_____

_____

_____

2. What was different about the authorities' plan to
apprehend Stephen from the one used to take Jesus?

_____

_____

_____

3. What is similar about the charges brought against
Stephen and the ones brought against Jesus. (See
Matthew 26:63–67)

_____

_____

_____

4. Why do you think Stephen started his "sermon" with
the story of Abraham?

_____

_____

_____

5. What is similar about the words of Stephen at his
death and the words of Jesus on the Cross? (See Luke
23:34)

_____

_____

_____

6. What later event do you think may have been the fruit of Stephen's prayer? (See Acts 9:1–5)

_____

_____

_____

7. Someone once asked what God had done for Stephen, he had after all been stoned to death? How would you answer that question?

_____

_____

_____

8. Both the cross of Christ and the death of Stephen bear eloquent testimony to the fact that when evil does its worst, God does his best. Can you trace any evidence of this truth in some incident or situation in your own life?

_____

_____

_____

Final Thoughts

When Pontius Pilot protested against the Jews' demands to crucify Jesus, they prayed, "Let his blood be on us and on our children." The Church has sometimes taken that statement literally at various points in history to justify its approval of the persecution of the Jewish people. They forgot that after the Jews uttered that dreadful statement, a little later Jesus prayed, "Father, forgive them, for they do not know what they are doing." Which prayer do you think God took the most notice of?

No matter how far we sometimes stray away from God, and may even call down the most dreadful consequences for our actions, it is never too late to ask for forgiveness

in the name of Jesus. Some of the greatest words of comfort that Jesus brings to those who turn to Him are, "Your sins are forgiven."

Closing Prayer

Father, we thank You for our time together. Thank You for everything we've shared together and the way You have acted in our lives. Forgive us for the times when we waver in our faith and help us to learn from the steadfastness shown by people like Stephen. Help us to have faith like that and to stand up for Jesus when it matters. In His name, Amen.

For Further Study

Being "full of the Spirit" is one thing; maintaining that fullness is another. Turn to Ephesians 5:18–21 to find the secret of maintaining a Spirit-filled life.

Paul makes it clear that we are saved by our faith – not by our good deeds. However, Paul also points out that our faith saves us for good deeds (see Philippians 2:12–16).

John
Loving One Another

Opening Prayer

Dear Father, We gather together in the last of the studies during Lent in the name of Your Son Jesus, to study another section of Your Word to us. We pray that You would open our eyes to see Jesus, open our ears to hear His words and open our hearts to receive Him in our meeting. Although we have seen a number of pictures of Jesus in our studies together, most of all we long to see Jesus Himself – lifted high and glorified in our lives. Bless our study as we seek to learn more about Him. In His name, Amen.

Eye Opener

One of the traditions from the early Christian Church was that John, as the last surviving apostle, spent his declining years as a very old man in the city of Ephesus in Asia Minor. When he grew too frail to walk to church, some of the young men would call for John, fasten poles to either side of his chair, and carry him through the city streets to the church meeting.

Each week, the preacher would ask John if he wished to address the congregation. and each time John would indicate that he did. The young men would carry him down the aisle to the front of the church and turn him to face the people. John would then smile and simply say, "Little children, love one another." He would then ask to be carried back again.

The next week, when John was asked if he wanted to say something to the people again, he affirmed that he did. Again he told them, "Little children, love one another."

Week after week John repeated his brief instruction. Finally one of the church leaders plucked up enough courage to ask John why he always told the people the same simple message.

"Because," said John, "if they do that, everything else will follow."

Ice Breaker

Try to describe to each other what happens to the value system of a person who falls head-over-heels in love.

Can you share with the group what happened to you when you fell in love.

Bible Reading

1 John 4:7–21

Dear friends, let us love one another, for love comes from God. Everyone who loves has been born of God and knows God. Whoever does not love does not know God, because God is love. This is how God showed his love among us: He sent his one and only Son into the world that we might live through him. This is love: not that we loved God, but that he loved us and sent his Son as an atoning sacrifice for our sins. Dear friends, since God so loved us, we also ought to love one another. No-one has ever seen God; but if we love one another, God lives in us and his love is made complete in us.

We know that we live in him and he in us, because he has given us of his Spirit. And we have seen and testify that the Father has sent his Son to be the Saviour of the world. If anyone acknowledges that Jesus is the Son of God, God lives in him and he in God. And so we know and rely on the love God has for us.

God is love. Whoever lives in love lives in God, and

God in him. In this way, love is made complete among us so that we will have confidence on the day of judgement, because in this world we are like him. There is no fear in love. But perfect love drives out fear, because fear has to do with punishment. The one who fears is not made perfect in love.

We love because he first loved us. If anyone says, "I love God," yet hates his brother, he is a liar. For anyone who does not love his brother, whom he has seen, cannot love God, whom he has not seen. And he has given us this command: Whoever loves God must also love his brother.

Introduction to John

The Galilean fishermen, of whom John was one, were notoriously tough and volatile characters who would not hesitate to speak out plainly on any occasion which concerned them. When we first encounter John in the Gospels, he seems to have a similar disposition. Along with his brother James, he blazed in anger at the Samaritans who would not give Jesus hospitality for the night. With good reason it seems, Jesus gave the brothers the name "Boanerges" – sons of thunder.

Again, when travelling to Capernaum, the disciples were found arguing as to who was the greatest among them. It is evident that ambition was fairly high on their list of priorities. James and John, perhaps encouraged by their mother, wanted the two top jobs in the kingdom and are considered by many commentators to be the two most ambitious disciples.

Yet it seems from the records in the Gospels, that John became the closest to Jesus of all the disciples (John never refers to himself by name in his Gospel, he just modestly calls himself "the disciple whom Jesus loved").

John occupied the place of honour at the Last Supper, where he could engage in close and intimate conversation with his Master. This close relationship between Jesus and John is revealed most clearly in the moments prior to Jesus' death, when he selects John to be the one who will have the responsibility fort the care of his mother Mary.

Although John was once a "son of thunder", it becomes obvious that Jesus changed him from a proud self-seeking zealot, into a kind, deeply loving and considerate person. In fact, the result of spending time in the presence of Jesus produces an amazing transformation in John, and he seems altogether a different disciple to the one who teamed up with Jesus in the beginning.

There can be little doubt that John was one of the greatest of all the apostles. In the Gospel which bears his name, John presents a view of Jesus which is quite different from that of the other three synoptic Gospels ("synoptic" means "a like view"). In John's account of Jesus' life, death and resurrection, the deity of Jesus shines through in majestic splendour.

In his Gospel, John portrays Jesus as the perfect Son of God. From all the miracles that Jesus did, John selects just seven to record – but they are the most God-like miracles that Jesus ever performed. Then John recounts seven occasions when people refer to Jesus as the "Son of God". Finally John reports the seven "I am ..." sayings of Jesus. ("I am" in Hebrew is "Yahweh" – the name of God.)

In Hebrew thinking the perfect whole number is seven, with "777" being the most perfect number of all (which explains, perhaps, why "666" is the most imperfect number!). John wants everyone to know that Jesus is perfect – as God is perfect.

The main lesson we learn from examining John's life is the fact that when someone walks constantly with Jesus, assimilating His words and obeying His instructions, then their obstinacy can turned into tenderness. Jesus can take imperfect people and through His influence, make them vessels of perfect love – changing their character to one in which love for God and love for others become the prime motivating forces. It is not by coincidence that John, the "son of thunder", became the "apostle of love" and from his letters, that love shines through.

The love that is at the heart of God, shines through Jesus' life in His dealings with other people. His care and concern, His gentleness and sympathy, His sacrifice and self-giving, all colour His relationships with those He came into contact with.

John ended up seeing that love was the most powerful force in the universe. Let's examine some questions that may allow us to see that this was the motivating force in Jesus' life too.

Questions

1. Why does John, in the first verse of our Bible reading, say we should love one another?

_____

_____

_____

2. How did God show His love among us?

_____

_____

_____

3. Why did God do this?

_____
_____
_____

4. Why do you think that if we love one another, God lives in us?

_____
_____
_____

5. One of Jesus' instructions to His followers was to be "perfect, therefore, as your heavenly Father is perfect" (see Matthew 5:48). This sounds impossible – but God would not tell us to aim for an impossible goal. So what do you think John is saying?

_____
_____
_____

6. Paul says that Jesus was "in very nature God" (see Philippians 2:6). What do you think was at the heart of this nature?

_____
_____
_____

7. How do you think it is possible to "love your enemies and pray for those that persecute you." (See Matthew 5:44)

_____
_____
_____

8. Is there anyone that you should be loving more?

_____

_____

_____

Final Thoughts

Jesus is God's picture for us of perfect love. Just as the motivation behind everything that God does is love, so Jesus is love in action. In every part of His life, Jesus' heart of love shines through. Love for God and love for mankind was behind everything that Jesus did when He was on earth, and everything that He does now in Heaven.

The Bible promises that one day those who have followed Jesus, will be changed into His likeness. This does not mean we will all look like Him in physical appearance but that we will all have our hearts changed into a likeness of Jesus' heart – a heart of love. It is in this way we will be made perfect – perfect in Jesus – and then we will live with the saints, with Jesus and with God in glory forever.

Closing Prayer

Almighty God, we have been privileged to glimpse pictures of your Son through the lives of other people from the Bible. In our lives too, we want to keep our eyes fixed upon Jesus. Help us to make Him the prime focus of all our studies and keep us walking with Him in the power of the Holy Spirit as we seek to follow Jesus – the true Author and Perfecter of our faith. Bless us now and in the future, surround us with Your love and keep us in Your care, for the sake of Jesus Christ, our Lord and Saviour. Amen.

For Further Study

As John was one of the twelve, he was chosen, not just to be a disciple of Jesus, but to be an apostle. The meaning of the word "apostle" is "one who is sent". A "disciple" is a much more general term, meaning a learner or student. (Notice the transition in Matthew 10:1 & 2.) Some believe that after the Church was established, apostles were no longer needed. Are there apostles functioning in the Church today?

John started out being very ambitious, and Paul says there is nothing wrong with this providing it is linked to the right goals (see Philippians 3:14–15). God has one ambition which supersedes all others (see Romans 8:29).

Leaders' Notes

These notes are designed as an aid to Group Leaders covering some of the potential points that could be covered during the Question sections of this publication. They do not claim to be exhaustive or to cover every question or view expressed by Group Members, and should be read as a guideline only.

Study One: Isaac – Willing to be Sacrificed

Question 1. Hebrews 11:19 tells us that Abraham believed in God's ability to resurrect his son from the dead. The parallel between this and God's resurrection of His Son, Jesus, from the dead, should be made.

Question 2. Abraham would "rejoice that he was to see the time of Jesus' coming", because what he believed about resurrection would actually come true in Jesus.

Question 3. There are many parallels that can be drawn out here. The main ones are: Abraham was a father with one true son, Isaac (although Abraham also fathered Ishmael through the slave girl Hagar, this was not the son that God wanted him to have). God is also a father with one true Son, Jesus.

Abraham did not hesitate to offer his one true son for sacrifice. God did not hesitate to offer His one true Son for sacrifice.

It was by Abraham's actions that his son was fastened to the place of sacrifice. It was by God's actions (not the Jews or the Romans) that Jesus was fastened to the cross.

Question 4. Again there are lots of parallels between the actions of Isaac and Jesus. The main ones are: Isaac carried the wood for the sacrifice on his back. Jesus carried the cross beam of the cross on his back.
Isaac willingly submitted to being positioned on the place of sacrifice although he could have easily used his superior physical strength to escape. Jesus willingly submitted to being placed on the cross although he could have called down thousands of angels to help Him escape.

Question 5. No angels stopped the crucifixion.

Question 6.
a. God provided a ram.
b. God provides Jesus, the Lamb of God.
c. God will always provide His Holy Spirit.

Question 7. Encourage Group Members to share their experiences of accepting Jesus.

Question 8. Encourage Group Members to give thanks to God for what He has done in their lives.

Study Two: Joseph – Redeeming the Lost

Question 1. Joseph's words, "I am Joseph" when he revealed himself to his brothers, parallel Jesus' words, "I am Jesus" when He revealed Himself to Saul (later Paul) on the road to Damascus. Both revelations led to a complete change of life for the hearers.

Question 2. God brought Joseph low before he was raised up to one of the highest positions in Pharaoh's kingdom, and given a title above most others. Jesus was brought low to the point of death before God raised Him to the highest place and gave Him a name that is above every name. That name is Redeemer.

Question 3. One common motivation was that both Joseph and Jesus accepted that God was directing their lives for His purposes, and that no matter what happened it was what God wanted of them.

Question 4. One answer could be greed. Judah saw the chance to make some profit out of Joseph's predicament, as Judas saw the chance to not have to repay the money he was taking from the disciples' common purse. Another answer could be that Judah took the opportunity to save his brother from a long lingering death, as Judas took the opportunity to force Jesus to show His real power.

Question 5. A number of instances could be quoted here. A few of these are when Jesus was not recognised by:
• the leaders of His day as the promised Messiah
• those people who shouted for His crucifixion as the Son of God
• the two disciples on the road to Emmaus
• His own disciples in Galilee when they saw a figure on the shore.

Question 6. The passage from Matthew tells us of The Transfiguration, when Jesus was revealed in His true splendour to Peter, James and John. Matthew reports that Jesus' glory was so bright it shone through His clothes as though they were transparent.

Question 7. Encourage the Group Members to share an instance in their experience when the glory of God shone through.

Question 8. Encourage Group Members to share in thanking God for giving Jesus to shed His light on their darkness.

Study Three: Esther – Saving her People

Question 1. Encourage Group Members to accept God's guiding hand is evident in the lives of Esther and Mordecai – and in their own lives too. He is is at work behind the scenes in every chapter of the Book of Esther.

Question 2. Esther and Jesus share in the unselfishness of their loving attitude towards others. Jesus made Himself "a servant" to people, although, as the Son of God, He had every right to expect people to serve Him.

Question 3. Jesus was born in a stable, not a palace – of humble parents (Joseph was a jobbing builder), not of the ruling royal family. He was an evacuee with His parents (the flight to Egypt), and then lived in a backwater town (Nazareth) under Roman rule. In His public ministry, Jesus experienced criticism about His teaching and miracles, threats to His life and health and finally public humiliation, whipping and death by crucifixion.

Question 4. Encourage Group Members to recall some of Jesus' statements about Himself, especially the "I am ..." sayings from John's Gospel:
I am the good shepherd
I am the way, the truth and the life
I am the gate
I am the vine
I am the bread of life
I am the resurrection and the life
I am the light of the world.

Question 5. The key to understanding the Book of Esther is the word "providence" – literally meaning "to provide in advance." God provided Esther to save the Jews of her day, just as God provided Jesus to save us today.

Question 6. Encourage Group Members to share times in their lives when minor details suddenly took on major meanings.

Question 7. Encourage Group Members to see that past "co-incidences" in their lives were, in fact "God instances".

Study Four: Mary – Trusting in God

Question 1. Encourage Group Members to think through the implications of being given great honour, but then being told of the sacrifices necessary for this.

Question 2. Encourage Group Members to recall times when they where in possession of privileged information about a situation or person. How did they use that information?

Question 3. Mary may well have been puzzled, even troubled by some of those Jesus chose to be His closest followers. Tough, blunt fishermen, tax collectors, and freedom fighters are not usually top of the list of friends a mother would want for her son. However, her acceptance of Jesus' choices shows the trust she gave Him.

Question 4. Again Mary could be forgiven for being troubled, even hurt, when having gone with her family to take charge of Jesus, He asked, "who are my mother and my brothers". Once more, her re-appearance later in the Gospel stories shows that any rejection she may have felt was overridden by the trust she placed in the Son of God.

Question 5. Encourage Group Members to share disappointments they may have felt when things didn't work out according to plan. Point out however that Mary's inner feelings are impossible to fully understand or analyse because they were unique.

Question 6. Encourage Group Members to talk about
times when, in times of despair and darkness, they fell
back on old friends to help them get through.

Question 7. If Group Members find it difficult to recall or
talk about their own sacrifices, encourage them to tell
about sacrifices they know other people have made.
(Read, for example, *Miracle on the River Kwai* by Ernest
Gordon, published by Fount.)

Question 8. Encourage Group Members to pray openly or
silently asking God if there are sacrifices He wants them
to make in their lives for Him.

Study Five: Stephen – Forgiving his Enemies

Question 1. Encourage discussion among Group Members
on what grace is and what power is in Christian terms.
Ask if the definitions given are the same in worldly terms.

Question 2. The plan of the Jewish authorities to apprehend Stephen was quite different from the one used to
take Jesus. There was no need to wait for Stephen to be
isolated from the crowd, or to secure the services of the
Temple guard. There was no need even to suppress any
semblance of violence. The circumstances of the day
enabled them to assume great boldness, and seizing a
favourable moment, to come upon Stephen either while
he was teaching in the synagogue or transacting his duties
as deacon.

Question 3. Both Stephen and Jesus were accused of blasphemy – the unforgivable crime in the eyes of the Jewish
authorities, for which the proscribed punishment was death.

Question 4. Abraham is regarded as the Father of the Jewish nation. Stephen takes the Sanhedrin back to the very beginning of their national story to show them God had planned the life and death of Jesus – even before He designated the Jews as His chosen people.

Question 5. Using similar words, both Stephen and Jesus asked that their tormentors and executioners be pardoned by God for their actions.

Question 6. It has been a conviction of the Church for centuries, that the conversion of Saul of Tarsus was the fruit of Stephen's prayer. The quenching of Stephen's light was the kindling of a brighter light for the illumination of the world.

Question 7. When Dr Joseph Parker was quite a young man he was used to discussing matters of faith outside the great ironworks on Tyneside in the north of England. One day someone challenged him to say what God had done for Stephen, as he'd been stoned to death. He answered, "What did God do for him? He gave him the power to pray for forgiveness for those that stoned him."

Question 8. Encourage Group Members to share experiences where God brought His light out of a dark situation in their life or in the lives of others.

Study Six: John - Loving One Another

Question 1. John says we should love one another, for love comes from God. In other words, the source of love in our world and in our lives is God. This is why John can confidently claim that "God is love".

Question 2. God showed us His love by sending Jesus. To make the point to the group, begin quoting John 3:16, "For God so loved the world that ...", and let the Group Members finish it.

Question 3. John says God did this because before we loved Him, God loved us. This is the most fundamental tenet of our Christian faith. Every major world religion claims that God is available to those who seek Him, like a book on a library shelf. Christianity is the only faith that claims God is dynamic in actively seeking us.

Question 4. If as John says, God is love, then expressing love to one another means that we are filled with God's quality. In this way God lives in us. God's principal motivating power is love, exactly the same motivation for the life and death of Jesus. If we make love the prime motive for everything that we do, then God truly lives in us.

Question 5. Following on from the previous question, we can only be as perfect as God in one aspect – love. When love is the one and only motive for all our thoughts, words and actions, then we can be perfect – perfect in love – just as God is. In the words of Charles Wesley:
  A heart in every thought renewed,
  And full of love divine;
  Perfect, and right, and pure, and good,
  A copy, Lord, of Thine.

Question 6. Hopefully, all Group Members will respond with the one word – "love".

Question 7. Encourage Group Members to read Romans 6:1–14. Paul talks about the principle of dying to sin and rising to new life in Christ Jesus. This means Christians can ask God to allow them to "die" to any hatred and anger and "rise" with new love in our hearts for our enemies.

Encourage discussion about how prayer can help us to appropriate the "dying and rising" principle for our lives.

Question 8. Encourage Group Members to think in silence for a minute or two about their answer to this question. They may find it more helpful if the Group Leader suggests open or silent prayer about this question, rather than open discussion.

Acknowledgement

CWR would like to express their sincere gratitude to the Trustees of the Wintershall Charitable Trust for their kind assistance in the production of this book by allowing the use of photographs from their play, *The Life of Christ*, featuring Simon Hemmingway who plays the part of Jesus.

Cover to Cover

The chronological *Cover to Cover* programme takes you through biblical events as they happened. This invaluable tool to discovering the Bible is available as a softback book, as a 6-part collection or as a 6-part subscription.

- 365 undated readings – start at any time of year
- An overview of each Bible book
- Helpful charts, maps, diagrams and illustrations
- Daily comments from the authors to encourage and challenge

Cover to Cover softback book. ISBN 1–85345–136–3
Content previously published as *Through the Bible Every Day in One Year*

£9.95 SOFTBACK BOOK
£9.95 6-PART COLLECTION
£9.95 ANNUAL SUBSCRIPTION

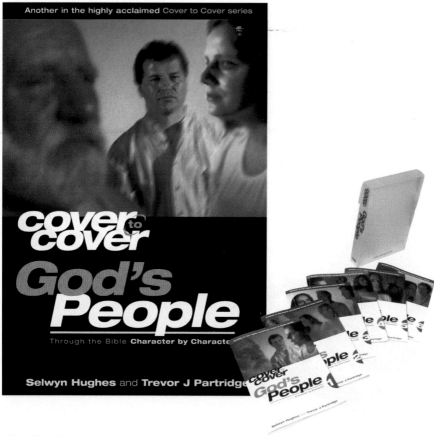

Another in the highly acclaimed Cover to Cover series

cover to cover

God's People

Through the Bible Character by Character

Selwyn Hughes and Trevor J Partridge

God's People

God's People is an exciting reading plan that introduces you to 58 fascinating Bible characters revealing the amazing relationship between God and humanity. The programme is available as a softback book, a 6-part collection or as a 6-part subscription.

- 365 undated readings – start at any time of year
- Selected readings taking approximately 10 to 15 minutes each day
- Key lessons on each character
- Daily comments from the authors to encourage and challenge

Content previously published as *Character by Character*
God's People softback book. ISBN 1–85345–160–6

£9.95 SOFTBACK BOOK
£9.95 6-PART COLLECTION
£9.95 ANNUAL SUBSCRIPTION